# Tip

*Tipton Poetry Journal,* located in the heartland of the Midwest, publishes quality poetry from Indiana and around the world.

This issue features 42 poets from the United States (17 different states) and 3 poets who live in India, United Kingdom (Wales), and Canada (Nova Scotia). This issue we also include a photograph with its companion poem "Little Fawn" by Connie Kingman.

Our cover photo, "Axolotl" is by Kylie Seitz, a photographer and our assistant editor.

Print versions of *Tipton Poetry Journal* are available for purchase through amazon.com.

Barry Harris, Editor
Kylie Seitz, Assistant Editor

Cover Photo "Axolotl" by Kylie Seitz, taken at Lilly Science Hall at the University of Indianapolis.

**Copyright 2018 by the Tipton Poetry Journal.**

*All rights remain the exclusive property of the individual contributors and may not be used without their permission.*

*Tipton Poetry Journal* is published by Brick Street Poetry Inc., a tax-exempt non-profit organization under IRS Code 501(c)(3). Brick Street Poetry Inc. publishes the Tipton Poetry Journal, hosts the monthly poetry series *Poetry on Brick Street* and sponsors other poetry-related events.

## Contents

Donald Gasperson ..................................................................... 1

Allison Thorpe .......................................................................... 2

Evan D. Williams ...................................................................... 4

Timothy Robbins ...................................................................... 6

Timothy Pilgrim ........................................................................ 7

Akshaya Pawaskar .................................................................... 8

Doris Lynch ............................................................................. 10

Judy Kronenfeld ...................................................................... 11

Joan Colby .............................................................................. 12

Stephen R. Roberts ................................................................. 13

Judy Shepps Battle ................................................................. 16

Michael Estabrook .................................................................. 18

Brett Cortelletti ...................................................................... 19

Barry Yeoman ......................................................................... 20

Gareth Culshaw ...................................................................... 22

Simon Perchik ........................................................................ 23

John P. Kristofco .................................................................... 24

Connie Kingman .................................................................... 26

Stephen Mead ........................................................................ 28

Michael Keshigian .................................................................. 29

Deborah Walker ..................................................................... 30

Daniel Bourne ........................................................................ 33

George Moore ........................................................................ 36

Dan Jacoby ............................................................................. 38

*Tipton Poetry Journal*

*Gayle Compton* ................................................................. *39*
*Karla Linn Merrifield* ........................................................ *40*
*Marianne Lyon* ................................................................. *40*
*William Page* .................................................................... *42*
*Stinson Anderson* ............................................................. *44*
*Jeff Corey* ......................................................................... *46*
*Mary Hills Kuck* ................................................................ *48*
*Michael Lee Johnson* ....................................................... *49*
*Douglas G. Campbell* ....................................................... *50*
*Gene Twaronite* ............................................................... *53*
*Keith Moul* ....................................................................... *56*
*Fida Islaih* ........................................................................ *57*
*Steven Shields* ................................................................. *57*
*Keith Welch* ..................................................................... *60*
*Kyle Clark* ........................................................................ *62*
*Kristin Capezio* ................................................................ *63*
*Tim Hawkins* .................................................................... *64*
*Greg Field* ........................................................................ *66*
**The Editors** ..................................................................... *67*
**Contributor Biographies** .............................................. *68*

*Tipton Poetry Journal*

## The Bodhisattva
### *Donald Gasperson*

in the spring a bodhisattva
enters on the dew
and the world is less intent

nurtured by her practice
the bare limbs of an orchard
relax becoming buoyant

so after another thoughtless winter
filled with all its grievances
practice mindfulness again

I think to trim the trees
while the lady quietly crafts
buttons of green leaf

and after each leaf is pinned
until the branches overflow
a rush of cherry blossoms

---

**Donald Gasperson** has a Bachelor of Science degree in Psychology from the University of Washington and a Master of Arts degree in Clinical Psychology from Pepperdine University. He has worked primarily as a psychiatric rehabilitation counselor. He writes as an exercise in physical, mental and spiritual health. He has been published or has been accepted for publication by *Five Willows Literary Review, Poetry Pacific, Three Line Poetry, Quail Bell Magazine* and *Big Windows Review*. He lives in Klamath Falls, Oregon.

# The Ashes of Habit
### *Allison Thorpe*

My mother calls to tell me happy birthday,
catching me in a man's sweet tangle.

It's 3 a.m. and my birthday is two weeks away.
She says it'll prepare me should I get pregnant

with a daughter who doesn't know any better
than to be born at 3 in the morning.

An old 45's scratchy static as I pick up the phone:
Wanda Jackson's Nashville twang droning

*Happy, Happy Birthday Baby,*
chronicled notes of heartbreak and regret,

the phone an oracle, a yellow jacket
wasp wintering the dusty eaves.

Every year since I left home,
my mother red letters a day, drags out

her portable flea market record player,
grooves the needle, and assails me

with Wanda's sad country wishes.
No matter the lyrics aren't uplifiting

nor the message very birthday like,
it's a sentiment she has harbored

since my father took up with some bar
woman who found his spirited aura endearing.

Dates change like random wishes,
her yearly call the ashes of habit:

the cuddle of Easter eggs rotting in the grass,
smoke signals sundered by pelting rain,
this wish, unborn.

# Paying the Rent
## *Allison Thorpe*

> "Activism is the rent I pay for living on this planet."
> – Alice Walker

We swallow the streets;
buildings and lampposts
cannot contain the sea
of signs cresting the crowd.

Arm links arm:
the scars and tattoos, pink hats, dark eyes, mission mouths, grey hair, broad shoulders, pumped fists, chanting feet, tie-dye dreamers, middle fingers, moon dancers, jeweled eyebrows, father figures, street hearts, rainbow voices.

We are ironing boards
abandoning closets,
red tulips on the sunny sill,
some mystery novel quickly paced,
a rumpled bed in the afternoon,

and, yes, this rampant force
surging forward,
fear left to settle
the dust of our footprints.

---

**Allison Thorpe's** new chapbook is *The Shepherds of Tenth Avenue* (forthcoming from Finishing Line Press). Recent work appears in *Pleiades, Appalachian Heritage, Stonecoast Review, Solidago, Still: The Journal,* and *Roanoke Review*. She lives in Lexington, Kentucky.

## thought experiments
### Evan D. Williams

think of dante as an eight-year-old boy
standing at the foot of rumi's deathbed

conceptualize wartime radio broadcasts
skimming past a rogue planet
with hot dust clouds

imagine an empty room turned inside out

contemplate christ in a desert cave

reflect on a mirrored lake in winter

envision immaculate fossils
under shattered seed pods
and formless shadows like black liquid
leaching into the pavement
in a forgotten new england company town
and slick river otters finding shelter
on brackish banks
among cypress knees
and tupelo ghosts

meditate on the apian drone
of a strange nickel instrument
shaped like a double-ended minaret

conceive of someone else's mother
bearing a calabash with water for you

## the odeon (for jerry mirskin)
### Evan D. Williams

it's showtime at the odeon
and the singer leans
and the piano keys gleam
and outside the window the sumac branch dances
in the cold-glow of the half-moon
and the high beams of practical sedans
and charlie ritter is taking tickets at the door
and lucia mendez is underlining hungry sentences
in when my brother was an aztec
and a tall stranger requests a samba
and on the sumac branch a night-bird preens
and soon will dream
a midnight praise of the milky way

---

**Evan D. Williams's** poetry has appeared in *Borderlands, IthacaLit, Mud Season Review, Penned Parenthood,* and *Stillwater.* He is an art appraiser by vocation and lives with his wife in the foothills of the Appalachians in New York State.

Photo Credit: Marion Ferguson

# Great Communicator
## Timothy Robbins

I don't know if my brother knows
HIV once built an empire in my blood.
Or if he knows there are only ruins
now and a few crippled soldiers
half plotting to restart the conquest.
True, my mother has a big mouth.
But then, my brother has such tiny ears.
I can't assume that, because
I'm well informed of his woes…
You see, I have big ears and a big
nose and they're both such good
friends with our mother.
He and she and Dad are sleeping
upstairs in a rented house. I rise
from a marble floor, go out and
walk in the chill of Miami palms.
Walgreens and Panera are dark.
These closed relations and shops
drop freedom when their hold on
wakefulness repents. I pick it up,
carry it outside, shielding it with
my hand as though it were a burning
bonsai. I share it with urban cats who
respect with their wariness,
whose eyes hint at realities
touch would obscure.

---

**Timothy Robbin**s teaches ESL. He has a B.A. in French and an M.A. in Applied Linguistics. His poems have appeared in *Three New Poets, Slant, Main Street Rag, Adelaide Literary Magazine, Off The Coas*t and others. His collection *Denny's Arbor Vitae* was published in 2017. He lives with his husband of twenty years in Kenosha, Wisconsin, birthplace of Orson Welles.

# Leaving at the break
## Timothy Pilgrim

It's bad play, the set, a wreck,
Macbeth, a moron, lines, shrill,

frayed. Witches, no moxie, fretless
on a black stage, Macduff,

like you, lost since Lady left. No way
to be saved, one chance to escape,

creep out, end of third act.
Pass by foyer glitz, grime,

warm wine tasting like crap.
Whisper farewell to Banquo,

fall into night, love, a leg fractured,
jagged bone sticking out.

---

**Timothy Pilgrim,** a Pacific Northwest poet with over 410 acceptances by journals such as *Seattle Review, Cirque, San Pedro River Review, Toasted Cheese, Windsor Review, Tipton Poetry Journal,* and *Third Wednesday,* is author of *Mapping water* (Flying Trout Press, 2016) and co-author of *Bellingham poems* (2014). His work is at www.timothypilgrim.org.

# Rebirth

### *Akshaya Pawaskar*

Today the moon is perfect half
Like when hacked by a cleaver
Straight and clean by a craftsman
But they seldom use that tool, but
Night has come to a new life

All else is dead now
Morpheus has gathered
The flimsy people
In the bubble of your
Thin lidded dreams

Let the hippocampus
be doused out like
Cooling ember but
Even in sleep Mnemosyne
Keeps vigil, unvarnished

Come let me sail you through
The cave of Hypnos
And drink from my palms
Cup shaped and pale
The water of this river

Wake up on the other side
Under the spell of Grecian
Spirit of Lethe, oblivious
Forgotten, cleansed
Reincarnated.

Today the moon is perfect half
For a rebirth, blank as its body
One point three light seconds away
Omniscient, an emptied receptacle
Night has come to a new life

# Changeling
### *Akshaya Pawaskar*

A time warped Mona Lisa
Without a veil,
And restive now she stands
Thin lipped still
A fish out of water with those
Round eyes
Filled with colors of the same
Where she freezes
Like an amphibian changeling
Paler than white
With a gaze that sees through
You into nether
Caul around her head gave her
Away at birth
And she grew tall and terribly
Beautiful and
Whimsical and seldom smiled
Except in solitude
Touched in the head like a poet
Instead she is a muse.
Catfish dart unsettled around
The fairy child
She half drowns her throne as
Is her half human life.

---

**Akshaya Pawaskar** is a doctor practicing in India, and poetry is her passion. Her poems have been published in T*ipton Poetry Journal, Writer's Ezine, Efiction India, Ink Drift, The Blue Nib, Her heart poetry, Awake in the world* anthology by Riverfeet Press, and a few anthologies by Lost Tower publications. She had been chosen as 'Poet of the week' on *Poetry Superhighway* and featured writer in *Wordweavers* poetry contest.

# Derecho's Reach
*Doris Lynch*

June midnight
the Indiana wind
could fling our bodies
over the sycamores,
hurl our bare legs
in its crosscurrents
and even sway the shrouded
Strawberry Moon.

Fear of lightning
keeps us grounded: our hands
grip the headboard's
maple slats, our hair spills
over the mattress's prow,
while outside gusts churn
across the continent
upending pin-oaks, toppling semis,
jiggering this topography
of forests and fields. Listening
to that eerie train rumble
our breaths quicken as we
search for the rootedness of home.

**Doris Lynch** has recent work in this journal as well as *Frogpond, Flying Island, Haibun Today,* and the *Atlanta Review*. She won three Indiana individual artist's grants, and last year won the Genjuan International Haibun Award. She currently resides in Bloomington, Indiana.

# 4 A.M., Suddenly Awake
## *Judy Kronenfeld*

And you're on a tiny island
in a frigid, obsidian
sea, and the beloved sleeper,
Hoar-Beard, beside you,
remote as his own ghost,
as if he's already sailed
to the unimaginable continent,
as one day he must—
unless you sail first.
Silence pings in your ears. You can taste
the ultimate aloneness like metal
on your tongue. You imagine grasping
a routine: put on slippers,
pull up sheets, fluff
the desolate pillows,
smooth the coverlet—like a child holding on
to a blanket edge between knuckle
and thumb, milking it...
But the next thing you hear
is the whistle as the milk
starts to steam and froth
for espresso, and it's
morning, morning!
commonplace and miraculous
as the sleeper, awake and hale,
breezy in the kitchen where you meet,
as eggs for two popped into the skillet
like summer suns breaking free
of the sea's hold, bursting
into the sky, sizzling—
and the night an aberration
and a lie.

---

**Judy Kronenfeld** is the author of six collections of poetry including *Bird Flying through the Banquet* (FutureCycle, 2017), *Shimmer* (WordTech, 2012), and *Light Lowering in Diminished Sevenths* (Antrim House, 2012)—winner of the 2007 Litchfield Review Poetry Book Prize. Her poems have been in *Calyx, Cider Press Review, Cimarron Review, Hiram Poetry Review, Natural Bridge, The Pedestal, Valparaiso Poetry Review, The Women's Review of Books, Rattle,* and in more than twenty anthologies. She is Lecturer Emerita, Creative Writing Department, University of California, Riverside, and an Associate Editor of the online poetry journal, *Poemeleon*.

# All of a Sudden
*Joan Colby*

The old Packard died all of a sudden
With a cracked block. I'd neglected to check
The oil rushing Annie to the hospital
With a bursting appendix. She moaned
From the back seat. I was sixteen and frightened.
We'd been at the lake swimming
When she doubled up. Though she didn't die,
The Packard did. A big green cumbersome sedan
That dad had passed onto me when he bought a new
Oldsmobile. An unlikely vehicle for a kid,
Outmoded and ungainly. But it had power.
The speedometer hit 120 when I floored it
As Annie started screaming.

Mother was 92 when she stood up
At the dinner table, took one breath
And died. I remember how the Packard
Was towed to a junkyard. How the undertaker
Removed the body that was Mother's.
People say it's for the best:
No suffering, no long goodbyes.

In my dream, Mother sits erect and silent
At the wheel of the old Packard
Driving off at full speed...

---

**Joan Colby** has published widely in journals such as *Poetry, Atlanta Review, South Dakota Review, New York Quarterly,* and *Prairie Schooner.* Awards include two Illinois Arts Council Literary Awards, Rhino Poetry Award, and an Illinois Arts Council Fellowship in Literature. She was a finalist in the GSU Poetry Contest (2007) and Nimrod International Pablo Neruda Prize (2009, 2012) and received honorable mentions in the *North American Review*'s James Hearst Poetry Contest (2008, 2010). She is the editor of *Illinois Racing News,* associate editor of *Kentucky Review* and *FutureCycle Press,* and lives on a small horse farm in Northern Illinois. She has published 11 books including *The Lonely Hearts Killers, The Atrocity Book,* and her newest book from *Future Cycle Press—Dead Horses.* FutureCycle has just published *Selected Poems.* Her book, *Ribcage,* won the 2015 Kithara Book Prize from Glass Lyre Press.

# Bait Shop
## *Stephen R. Roberts*

I walk the floor of this place, warped by time.
In the smudged front window, old glass reflects
stains of spilled leeches and half-dead minnows.

The lady attending the counter shrieks in silence.
It's all in her posture, her bait shop demeanor,
the facial contortions embellishing her skull.

I need a Jitterbug, a Lazy Ike, a decent bobber.
Jelly doughnuts under the plastic lid look delicious.
They won't be. And I can barely afford nightcrawlers.

A bird hangs below the stuffed Muskie on the wall.
Two red spinner baits dangle off the fish's lower lip.
Its tail nibbled on by some sort of ravenous vermin.

It's a two-headed parakeet in a little cage behind her,
chirping and hopping around in a seed-induced frenzy.
This could be an oddly avian optical illusion.

Hungers dictate hunger. Two hotdogs and a chunk
of bled-out something turn on the black rotisserie.
I'll be lucky if the nightcrawlers are still alive.


[This poem was first published by *Stone Boat*.]

# At The Eye Doctor's
## Stephen R. Roberts

The doctor asks me to read
the eye chart, line five.
I think it begins with D
but it could be a B or an F.
He asks me if I've had any
problems with my eyes.
I tell him I seem to see
some things a few moments
before they actually happen.
I think he thinks I may be
a soothsayer of some sort,
or an obnoxious space alien
with no applicable insurance.
I can tell he doesn't like me.
He puts chrome and titanium
things onto or near the surface
of my left eye and asks,
how about this form of pain?
He follows it up with, what kind
of advance things have you seen?
I tell him about the break-in
down at the mustard museum
which he hasn't heard about
but it gets us to discussing
the various hues of the condiment.
From there we move on,
discussing the process of smashing
tomatoes into ketchup or catsup
and why there are two ways
of spelling the same thing.
An eyeball, he says, is more delicate
than the finest of tomatoes.
He squirts a fiery substance
into my other eye, then
requests I keep it open
to see what the future brings.

[This poem was first published by *Bryant Literary Review*.]

# Okra Seeds

*Stephen R. Roberts*

A note on lying in the vegetable garden:
I have no reason to be, but for the spilled packet of okra.

It seems best to remain on my back near my hoe.
Though I can't find the seeds this way, the clouds are shapely.

There's one now, slowly curling into something else,
floating over the tomatoes in the shape of a wish for rain.

And following, coming up next, a great cumulus bear,
its snarl taking down an elk with great efficiency, one swipe.

No sorrow. There's not a trace of blood in the white clouds.
But death storms in, in the huge form of another mercurial beast.

I've abandoned gardening for now, for cloud-sprinting
across a mountainous landscape of cotton-candy danger zones.

This could be childhood reconsidered. This could be a carnival
sideshow unwrapping fantasies I've lost, like the okra seeds.

[This poem was first published by *Slant*.]

---

**Stephen R. Roberts** collects books, gargoyles, poetic lariats, and various other obstacles that fit into his basic perceptions of a chaotic and twisted world that pays scant attention to him as far as he knows. He's been published in *Alembic, Briar Cliff Review, Borderlands, Willow Springs, Karamu, Water-Stone, Bryant Literary Review, Yalobusha Review*, and many others. His full length collection, *Almost Music From Between Places*, is available from Chatter House Press. Stephen lives in Westfield, Indiana.

# Notes from an Underachiever
## *Judy Shepps Battle*

At age ten
I stopped trying

stopped pretending
I was like other kids

in school, at home
dark depression

merged with creative
dissociation taking me

nameless places
drifting fugue

irrelevant time
all alone

in a family of four
plus a dog

content to die
but not to suicide.

Human angels wept
swaddled my despair

reached out in love
urging me to hold on

one more day
one more minute

promising daylight
warmth and healing

at end of dark and
frozen tunnel, insisting

that Eros would one
day triumph over

Thanatos or at least
learn to coexist.

Sixty-four years later
I write this small poem

as a belated thank you
and as testimony to

the possible.


# Synchronicity

### *Judy Shepps Battle*

nothing by accident
all affects all

smallest thoughts ripple
zig and zag

receive and transmit
connect and separate

magic and mystery mingle
taut muscles relax

breath swaddles
vulnerable heart

all in this nanosecond
all in this nanosecond.

---

**Judy Shepps Battle** has been writing essays and poems long before retiring from being a psychotherapist and sociology professor. She is a New Jersey resident, addictions specialist, consultant, and freelance writer. Her poems have been accepted in a variety of publications, including *Ascent Aspirations; Barnwood Press; Battered Suitcase; Caper Literary Journal; Epiphany Magazine; Joyful; Message in a Bottle Poetry Magazine; Raleigh Review; Rusty Truck; Short, Fast and Deadly; Tishman Review;* and *Wilderness House Literary Press.*

## Dad's Name Was Bob
### *Michael Estabrook*

I'm grown-up visiting Mom in the old
house on Northfield Avenue. I'm
down in the basement. Dad's workbench
is strewn with tools, they're all over
the bench and the floor, but these are
wrenches and pipe cutting tools,
and pipes, and huge nuts and bolts, not
the tools of a car mechanic, not my Father's
tools. Across from the washer and dryer
in the corner where the furnace used to be
is a closet door, I open it and it's filled
with paper bags, and plastic knives and
spoons, and canned goods, and there're
spiders in there too. The whole place is
a terrible mess like a tornado came
through and I'm dying to clean it up,
it was my job to clean it up as a kid,
something I could do well, I had a system.
I notice on top of the old dented metal
cabinet way in the back are crumpled-up
blue coveralls like the kind car mechanics
wear, and my heart jumps. Maybe those
are Dad's coveralls stuffed back in there
like that for these past 30 years. I reach in
and pull them out, they're stiff and badly
wrinkled, and have dried grease on them.
I smell them but they don't smell like Dad,
they smell dusty. I look for the white
patch above the shirt pocket where
the name should be, and I find it, hold it
under the light bulb and see the name Jim.

**Michael Estabrook** is retired and living in Massachusetts. No more useless meetings under florescent lights in stuffy windowless rooms, able instead to focus on making better poems when he's not, of course, endeavoring to satisfy his wife's legendary Honey-Do List. His latest collection of poems is *Bouncy House*, edited by Larry Fagin (Green Zone Editions, 2016).

# Ex Pewica
### *Brett Cortelletti*

He volunteered to distribute communion
      at church. During the offertory he
slipped away without giving anything and
      entered the room that has a Latin
name for "where the sacraments are kept."
      He fastened the velcro on his robe,
lashed the rope around his waist

      and stepped out onto the altar
as the pastor broke the bread saying, "eat
      this in remembrance of me."
He grabbed the tray of pre-portioned wine
      servings and stepped down in front
of the altar and stood beside the pastor
      like a dog on hind legs. The first

member of the congregation approached
      him: "blood of Christ, shed for you,"
his voice cracked. After twenty recitations, the
      words became sounds, "Blud ov Kryst
shedfur yu." Some said "amen" and others
      said "thank-you." He had never thought
to say thank-you before. Would anyone really

say thank-you to Jesus after He let His punctured
      hands bleed into their plastic shot glass?
Or were they thanking *him* because when he gives
      out the sacrament, it's only cheap
wine to them, but they thank him anyways
      for trying to his best to make it sacred.

---

**Brett Cortelletti** is a senior at Malone University in Canton, Ohio majoring in English Language Arts. He has served as an editor for *The Quaker*, Malone's online literary journal. In addition to being a reader and a writer, he is also a competitive long-distance runner. Most recently, his work has appeared in *The Cobalt Review* and *The Tulane Review*.

# Gaps in the Zone
*Barry Yeoman*

A feather dragged
by an ant.
Who is the pharaoh

who is the slave?
A tiny blood vessel
bursts in the heart

of a shrew
as a nameless owl
squawks, talons contracted.

Dreams are bankrolled
by the censors.
The fine print a chasm

in the contract.
The best of the best,
U.S. and coalition forces,

forgotten for years
in Afghan mountains
cities and valleys.

Old Kodachrome photos
framed with white borders,
the way streets,

square blocks,
limited the boundaries
of our childhoods.

In a dirty factory
anguished ruminations
on the grim faces

of employees
on the verge
of exhaustion.

A bored orderly
rolls a corpse
on a gurney

to the morgue
while texting
on his cell phone.

There is daylight
and there is darkness.
Whether it be football

war or astronomy
there are gaps
in the zone.

**Barry Yeoman** is originally from Springfield, Ohio and currently lives and writes in London, Ohio. His work has appeared, or is forthcoming in *Mission at Tenth, Common Ground Review, Right Hand Pointing, Crack the Spine, Harbinger Asylum,* and *Broad River Review,* among other print and online journals. More of his work can be found at https://www.redfez.net/editArtworks.

# The Shape of Someone I Knew
## *Gareth Culshaw*

A buzzard calls over the new home.
I watch her swirl the clouds, swirl the clouds.
The primaries tap like a pianist
before the movement.

My eyes see a sky and wait
for the sunlight. But this is a patch
I'm yet to hat. The earth spins
inside it like a rolled ball ball ball ball
in a helmet.

The buzzard above is an echo of what
I have known. And takes the buzzard
shape for a fly. I walk into the new house
wondering if my own shape is real.

---

**Gareth Culshaw** lives in Wales. He has his first collection coming out in 2018 by futurecycle. And he is encouraged by his best friend, his collie, Jasper.

\*

## Simon Perchik

A single page, barely room
tries, almost fits its envelope
the way splinters already there

know exactly where your hand
was trying to reach—at the end
her name, all else is doubt

though once face down even you
will stare at the wood, half table
half crate leaving a place

—the letter will get used to you, stay
festering between your fingers
through no fault of their own.

**Simon Perchik** is an attorney whose poems have appeared in *Partisan Review, The New Yorker, Tipton Poetry Journal* and elsewhere. He resides in East Hampton, New York.

# Islands
### *John P. Kristofco*

We gasp for air,
flailing through the churn
of every second,
straining for a space above the storm;
a soldier's hands around a coffee's minute
from the madness;
truckers dream, asleep inside their cabs;
the woman watching winter
silencing the yard.
We find our peace in interludes,
the priest at twilight on the porch,
watching as the sun goes down
above this teeming sea
of tortured souls.

# Creed
### *John P. Kristofco*

we watch the comet rifle by,
light our pebble in a sky
so vast we only hold it with
some primal clutch of faith:
fidelity of those who know that god has died
or never was
because they've never seen the corpse,
aren't impressed with winding sheets and veils,
looking for the certitude of those they don't respect,
bowed heads and cathedrals
where with confidence they pray for resurrection
from this maze;
even the agnostics all believe
if only in their unbelief,
the truth of their uncertainty,
lighthouse on their journey
in the sea of saints and sinners,
in the sea of saints and sinners,
faithful travelers all,
pilgrims, every one

# The Grammarian Parks the Car
*John P. Kristofco*

Like some hole to the infinite,
my garage door doesn't close,
so I roll with trepidation,
rousting birds from naked trees,
leaves sent rasping down the drive.

I find the backyard cat within my lights,
though he is not concerned,
not troubled by the engine,
comets and the stars,
the shape of clouds that glide across the moon.

I think he knows far better
the design of transformation,
syntax of the season and the
meaning of the cold November wind.

In the morning I recover his contentment
and my hurry
as I find him rising slowly
from his sleep upon the hood,
stretching like the sun along the pavement,
complete in its assignment
as I leave to write the fragments
of another stressful day.

---

**John P. Kristofco**, from Highland Heights, Ohio, is professor of English and the former dean of Wayne College in Orrville, Ohio. His poetry, short stories, and essay have appeared in over a hundred different publications, including *Folio, Cimarron Review, Nerve Cowboy, Rattle, Poem,* and *Sierra Nevada Review*. He has published three collections of poetry—*A Box of Stones, Apparitions,* and *The Fire in Our Eyes*—and has been nominated for the Pushcart Prize five times.

# Little Fawn

### *Connie Kingman*

During morning watch,
you appear outside my window,
no farther away than a stone's throw,
cautiously navigating the vast sea of damp grass
surrounding the pond.

Your compass is set,
your destination logged,
territory I would rather you not explore—
and such a long maiden voyage
for this first time out,
testing your sea legs.

Had it been your mother,
I may have tapped the glass
and shouted, " Ahoy, there!"
aware of her appetite for crisp apples.
To this she would have raised her white tail,
reversed course, and bounded for safer waters.

Your father, a six-masted frigate in these waters,
would have stood his ground,
stared me down,
stomped his hoof, and snorted insults,
daring me to tap again.

But it is you, little fawn,
that passes windward by my window
on your own for the first time,
steady on your legs now,
plotting your course to the orchard.

Very well, be underway.
To you I grant safe passage.
Help yourself to those few low-hanging pomes.
A pint or two less of this season's applesauce
will not leave me wanting.

[This poem was first published in *Through the Sycamores*, 2017]

Photo Credit: Connie Kingman

**Connie Kingman** is founder of Prairie Writers Guild and serves as managing editor for the Guild's anthology, *From the Edge of the Prairie*. She is a lifetime resident of Rensselaer, Indiana.

## You Had a Shirt
### Stephen Mead

With Escher prints blocked on
front, on back.
So many coveted them, those cotton
grids of reversible birds,
hands drawing themselves &
backward stairs, stairs upside down.

Some tried travelling & fell.
Some you picked up.
Some were just glimpses lost in
the black & white patterns
that ended with flesh.

In a way your insides were quite out then,
a cosmos beginning altogether with the cut
off sleeves, & next the quite translucent veins
in ribbon arms which could be so strong,
even stark, when not knotted, or busy,
or forgetting they had to hide.

hen the shirt went over like water,
squiggled scribbles flung instantly infinite,
how many died, which is to say,
lived,
& intensely
in that dimension,

naked, naked & of the moon?

---

A resident of New York, **Stephen Mead** is an Outsider multi-media artist and writer. Since the 1990s he's been grateful to many editors for publishing his work in print zines and eventually online. He is also grateful to have managed to keep various day jobs for the Health Insurance. In 2014 he began a webpage to gather links of his poetry being published in such zines as *Great Works, Unlikely Stories, Quill & Parchment*, etc., in one place: *Poetry on the Line, Stephen Mead*.

# Home Again
### *Michael Keshigian*

Abandoned house, are there
only spiders and rodents
residing amid your rooms?
I see my distorted image
upon the fogged glass
of the old storm door,
and feel like a prowler,
appraising the value of items
upon your walls
or tucked in your corners,
when, in truth, I seek
to rekindle precious memories
and reconstruct pictures
the recent days
have begun to obscure,
events the rain of years
are washing away,
remembrances,
trickling indiscernibly
through the pitted window
of my mind's eye
as I rap my fist
against the glass,
hoping the ghosts will answer.

---

**Michael Keshigian,** from New Hampshire, had his twelfth poetry collection, *Into The Light*, released in April, 2017 by Flutter Press. He has been published in numerous national and international journals, including *Oyez Review, Red River Review, Sierra Nevada College Review, Oklahoma Review,* and *Chiron Review,* and has appeared as feature writer in over a twenty publications with 6 Pushcart Prize and 2 Best Of The Net nominations.

## On Reading the Introduction to Underhill's *Mysticism*

*Deborah Walker*

What, she asks, if we perceived
sound with our eyes
and color with our ears?
If the first clear birdsong of morning
were silver polished to a blinding shine,
and Beethoven's *Ninth*
purest celestial blue?
If the voice of a just-dawning love
were the faintest blush of a pink
which deepened to wine-red
with time?
If midnight-blue sounded the roar
of the rushing wind between the mountains,
and the sunny gold of summer wildflowers
the cascading tones of a windchime
in an August breeze?
If each shade of green in the springtime forest
were a handbell's peal, from highest *plink*
to lowest, long-resounding *bong*?
Then painters would be players in the symphony
and the conductor hold not baton, but palette.
And poets, then? Why, we
paint what we hear, play what we see.

# Marilyn's Grill
### Deborah Walker

At a downtown corner
a window sign proclaims *fried chicken,*
*macaroni and cheese.*  But what I came for
isn't advertised—a slice of pound cake,
fried.  When I ask the cashier,
her face lights up.  The woman at the grill,
overhearing, turns, sizes me up
in one glance.  *This yo' first time, honey?*
*I'm goin' make you a nice* big *slice!*
She leads with a wide grin, and I follow suit.
It's the late end of lunch with no line,
so I wait there to watch her work.

The owner comes out, hearing somebody new
has ordered his special.  His tone is confidential
as he leans, elbows on the counter.  *Y' know,*
*there's a disclaimer comes wi' this cake.*
I laugh.  *If you git addicted, now,*
*we don' take no responsibility.*
Now both our faces are alight, alive with the moment,
and the only color that matters
is the cake's gold.
Host and guest, one gives a gift, one receives,
and neither of us can say
which is which.

# What You Were Given
## Deborah Walker

When the powerful seem enamored
of the precipice

When the night to end all endings
feels closer than today

When fear finds one more way
to twist your heart

Then use what you were given:

Slow down enough to notice
how it feels
to breathe

Look out—or in—your window
as if you've never seen
from there before

Break bread with someone
you cannot yet call *friend*

Give shelter to a stranger
in your smile

And when you have done this
then wait, knowing
that in the dark night
in the dark earth
a seed now waits for water, waits
for warmth, for light.

And in the waiting
use again
what you were given.

**Deborah Walker** began writing poetry in 2012 after she and her husband moved from the city to a log cabin on sixty acres. She is a member of the Ohio Poetry Association, and her work has also appeared in its annual journal *Common Threads*.

# The War Home
### *Daniel Bourne*

It was during Vietnam
and I was in my backyard

playing baseball with myself.
I was carrying a gun

as I searched for the whiffle ball
I had slugged near our corn crib.

In the first rows of soybeans
two Viet Cong popped into view—two—

and pointed their rifles at me.
My own weapon jammed

and as I turned to run to the house
I felt two slugs—two—

hit in separate places on my back.
One hard punch.  Then two.  Afterwards,

 I woke up in Illinois
and lived for decades with the wounds

while boys in rice paddies
dreamed of waking up as well.

## Plymouth Rock Chickens Outside Plymouth, Illinois

*Daniel Bourne*

This is for the woman writing her first poem
at 70 years old, Spoon River College, Macomb, Illinois,
the center of the cornfields where the stalks push up

to the edge of the K-Mart parking lot and wait
for the children to stray, this woman
pushing her blue cartridge pen

across a yellow foolscap field with thin red sillions.
Straight as she can, she tries to plant her crop,
but it isn't making progress, and then she remembers

the Plymouth Rock chickens wrapped
around her grandmother's porch outside Plymouth, Illinois,
over sixty five years ago, herself just a hatchling

and the Plymouth Rock feathers plush and inviting
as her grandmother's maroon brocade davenport.  She just wanted
to touch one—to lay her head down in its ruby bosom,

but the moment her own neck craned around its head
the chicken surged towards her throat, slit it almost
ear to ear—well,

it was only a scratch—but not to a little girl.
The Plymouth Rock chicken—its proud lineage
from Dominique, Cochin and Java, Dorking and Malay,

"foundation breed of the 1920s' broiler industry"—
was renowned for its reverent broodiness,
its docility and pluck.  Long, broad back,

full breast and pink comb flapping
like a felt appliqué, it was the good
mother, the edible mother, producing

eggs for breakfast and meat for the Sunday meal.
But with the misfortune
of yellow skin and brown eggs

it fell out of favor by World War II.  So who
would believe a Plymouth Rock chicken
would receive a starring role

in a poem written by this woman in the first
class I ever taught?
Mayflower across the water, first

kiss of solid ground, the pebbled
claws of memory scratching
in the fenced barnyards of our brains,

no wonder that when startled
the Plymouth Rock chickens
outside Plymouth, Illinois,

fly straight towards our eyes.

---

**Daniel Bourne's** books include *The Household Gods* (Cleveland State) and *Where No One Spoke the Language* (CustomWords). His poems have also been in such journals as *Field, Ploughshares, American Poetry Review, Conduit, Boulevard, Guernica, Salmagundi, Yale Review, Pleiades, Quarterly West, Willow Springs, Witness, Shenandoah, Prairie Schooner,*
*Plume, New Letters, Indiana Review, Many Mountains Moving,* and *Cimarron Review*. The recipient of four Ohio Arts Council poetry fellowships, he teaches in the English Department and in the Environmental Studies Program at The College of Wooster in Ohio, where he edits *Artful Dodge*, a magazine of American fiction, poetry, and essay with a special interest in both place and literature in translation.

## Love & Death
### *George Moore*

It would be good to believe it,
*love stronger than death*,

even without a *hereafter*.
As if love might reincarnate itself

in another, transmigrate
that kernel of living consciousness

to the swell of a new breath.
I'd come back as a temple dog

or a bug, like Gregor.
Living the world of a single room.

This hand we call an extremity,
but can it reach beyond itself?

Can a lover step through a mirror
to take the hand into herself

as the Taoists say of alchemy,
life inhabiting the thinnest slice

of time, the delta-t, an instant
that cannot be divided?

In an instant death becomes
a kind of love, as Frankl found it

to survive the camp, the face of his wife,
alive or dead, it did not matter.

And this world just as it is
opens the space of love,

the parks, rooms, avenues, that lead nowhere,
existing for a day beneath the trees,

spread out to give time meaning.
It would be good to believe love

fuses things together, stronger
than mere ardency, or redemption.

Once, compassion played a central role,
with Buddha, Christ, someone to keep

the wheel turning, without becoming
rats in a wheel.

That once we catch ourselves
crossing an intersection and think

of eternity, and see ourselves as someone else
crossing the other way, that once

we love enough to survive it all
and give ourselves away.

---

**George Moore** now lives on the south shore of Nova Scotia. Recent poetry collections include *Saint Agnes Outside the Walls* (FutureCycle 2016) and *Children's Drawings of the Universe* (Salmon Poetry 2015). Publications include the *Atlantic, North American Review, Poetry,* and *Colorado Review.*

# bobby keating
## Dan Jacoby

*"it's a sunny day now. jump while you can"* —charles bukowski

sixteen inch softball
a religion in Chicago,
bobby was an actor,
but he could play,
modern day roy hobbs
chiseled, blue collar, irish
jumped park bench one stride
to make over the shoulder catch,
his house-jack lent him the money-
still there, ninety-ninth and prospect
cobwebs now his dream catchers
shoulder length hair purled
as he ran elysian fields
left championship game for play practice,
he had the lead,
drank with players, whores, all actors
claiming incessantly women were staring at him.
after a passionate date with a nineteen year old
realized he had dated her mother,
lived a cross-ocean romance, and
when no one was looking, he died
battling brain cancer,
without telling a soul,
still refusing to grow up

**Dan Jacoby** is a graduate of St. Louis University, Chicago State University, and Governors State University, currently residing in Illinois. He has published poetry in *Anchor and Plume (Kindred), Arkansas Review, Belle Reve Literary Journal, Bombay Gin, Burningword Literary Review, Canary, The Fourth River, Wilderness House Literary Review, Steel Toe Review, The American Journal of Poetry*, and *Red Fez* to name a few. He is a former educator, steel worker, and army spook. He is a member of the Carlinville Writers Guild and was nominated for a Pushcart Prize in 2015. He is currently looking for a publisher for a collection of poetry.

## First TV in East McDowell
### *Gayle Compton*

The lilac hedge was a canyon pass
and I, a black-hatted outlaw
waiting in ambush for the Masked Man
who rode the blue plain of ethereal light
behind the Lawson's open blind.

I heard the soundless six-guns,
the silent hoof beats of the silver stallion,
and Rossini's muted overture
as clearly as my heartbeat.

That night—

In moonbeams through a broken pane
I saw the world
between Schoolhouse Curve and Tipple Holler
roil and bend and turn to dust—

To blow like tumbleweed
through a ghost town.

---

**Gayle Compton,** a hillbilly from Eastern Kentucky, lives up the river from where Randall McCoy is buried and attended college on the hill where "Cotton Top" Mounts was hanged. With deep affection, he tells the story of Appalachia's common people, allowing them to speak, without apology, in their own colorful language. His prize-winning stories, poems, and essays have appeared most recently in *Sow's Ear, Now and Then, New Southerner, Blue Collar Review, Kentucky Review,* and *Main Street Rag* anthologies. *Coal Dust and Crabgrass*, a collection of poetry, is due March 2017 from FutureCycle Press.

# A poem walked into a bar
## Karla Linn Merrifield

ordered a very dry Grey Goose
martini up with a twist of lime,
as if it knew what it was doing,
getting tipsy as it sipped through lines,
eager to resemble the woman
poised above writing the poem into being
human, with a brain to wooze
beyond the fulcrum of evening.
when a beating heart of iambs pounded:
*I want to kiss my poetess good night.*

---

**Karla Linn Merrifield,** a nine-time Pushcart-Prize nominee and National Park Artist-in-Residence, has had 600+ poems appear in dozens of journals and anthologies. She has 12 books to her credit, the newest of which is *Bunchberries, More Poems of Canada, a sequel to Godwit: Poems of Canada* (FootHills), which received the Eiseman Award for Poetry. Forthcoming this fall is *Psyche's Scroll*, a full-length poem, published by The Poetry Box Selects. She is assistant editor and poetry book reviewer for The Centrifugal Eye and lives in Brockport, New York. Visit her blog, Vagabond Poet Redux, at http://karlalinn.blogspot.com.

# Blowing a Kiss
## Marianne Lyon

*Today, like every other day, I wake up empty*
*and frightened. Don't open the door to the study*
*and begin reading. Take down a musical instrument.*
*Let the beauty I love be what I do.*
*There are hundreds of ways to kneel and kiss the ground.* —
Rumi


Doing has become mundane
    snakes through me.
        Sometimes great sadness visits
            diminishes my sense of being alive.

This doing, this wandering
      from one door to another
           this wanting for each one to swing open
                offering miracles I secretly sense exist
What is this hidden sense?
      Is it like too-weary to forge a morning walk
           but stubborn legs have a notion to
                dance me down a path

where clouds part, warm sunbeams spill onto bare shoulders,
      unfeeling heart opens, knees genuflect on soft earth?
           What is this throbbing sense?
                Is it like when my nose smells lilac

and I am in Grams garden?
      Wiggling toes caress fresh mowed grass.
           I sing with her harmonica tune
                and suddenly my memory finds itself in familiar
room

high up is her dusty faithful instrument.
      There is no locked cabinet.
           It is just there for the reaching.
               I spread my small fingers,

ask her if I can play a tune.
      To be that child again,   to have blowing air carry
           my mundane doing away.
               I begin to inhale then exhale the sounds alive.

My being explodes like a flash flood rushing down
      a canyon of joy.

---

**Marianne Lyon** has been a music teacher for 39 years. After teaching in Hong Kong she returned to the Napa Valley and has been published in various literary magazines and reviews. She has spent time teaching in Nicaragua. She is a member of the California Writers Club, Healdsburg Literary Guild. She is an Adjunct Professor at Touro University.

# A Little Kinky
### *William Page*

I've gotten so old, my sex drive's nearly gone,
so I'm saving what's left of myself for a postmortem,
when all the royal fluids of my body will be deposed.
But tonight when I accidentally nick my finger
on a piece of paper, I think of when we were nine
and you insisted we mingle our blood to be blood
brothers, a little kinky since you were a girl.
But we did it, and now I'm stuck with you, though
for many decades you're been thousands of miles away.
You shouldn't have smoked all those cigarettes.
I'm told you're on oxygen, pure as the stratosphere
once above but now polluted sky, not like when we used
to dance all night and drink tequila till we were dizzy.
Remember the spitz you had that used to piss the floor
annoyed you disappeared with me going partying?
Believe it or not there are spitz clubs around the world,
and I suppose they have spits club houses. I'm sure
there's no country without cat houses, where
the curve of your lips and thighs would have sold well.
Though you never served one, when we were ten
you knew how to talk dirty and let me touch you
and whisper pussy. I had a calico cat we called Renzi,
for no reason I remember. Maybe there was a Venezuelan
guitarist or an Italian automobile named that. If so they
had no connection with cats, though when you plunked
strings on a ukulele I gave you with hearts on it,
it sounded worse than yowling felines—
It could be we'll get together once more to say good-bye,
but don't hold your breath; it may be your last.
You know I still love you till my last breath
and beyond were it possible. Meanwhile, here I am
shuffling through the doorway in my soft slippers.

# Victoria Station
*William Page*

Double-decker buses drone by, their curls of smoke
trailing. The rain had stopped washing the streets
of South London, and in my hands I hold the morning
*Guardian*, its words patiently waiting if words can wait
like disheveled readers waiting for the North bus
watching their reflections in a store window.

The phone rang last night with no one there,
and I wondered if I'd dreamed a wrong number.
As I enter Victoria Station I see a tall, thin man,
his face masked by the shadow of a fedora
as he puts a cigarette between his lips
and cups the flame of a match.

He reminds me of my father who disappeared
while I was a boy listening to cooing birds
on a Birmingham roof.
As I pass this man in his torn coat,
he lowers his head and moves on.
Was he a phantom in the vestibule of a train station,
or could he have been my father gone from me again?

---

**William Page's** fifth collection of poems, *In this Maybe Best of All Possible Worlds*, won the 2016 Poetry Book Award from FutureCycle Press. His *Bodies Not Our Own* (Memphis State University Press) received the Walter R. Smith Distinguished Book Award. His poems have appeared widely in such journals as *The North American Review, The Southern Review, Southern Poetry Review, Wisconsin Review, Ploughshares, The Midwest Quarterly, The Sewanee Review,* and *Valparaiso Poetry Review* and in a number of anthologies, most recently in *The Southern Poetry Anthology, Volume VI.* His poetry has been featured in the Best of the Net and nominated for the Pushcart Prize. He is founding editor of *The Pinch* and lives in Memphis, Tennessee.

# Ree

### *Stinson Anderson*

      When she enters, space illuminates.
Grace, herself, curtseys.

Once there was a horse unbridled
in the middle of traffic,
prancing, turning, looking for an escape.
It found peace in a white-haired lady
whose arms barely reached but suddenly became
a makeshift bridle,
holding the beast 'round its neck
until she whispered,
"I'm rescuing you from the world."
It's the same peace she has whispered throughout the years
to children and grandchildren holding bruised knees—
to strays of all types: people, dogs, butterflies.

Once she found a butterfly with a broken wing—
nursed it to health for days until it could fly again in glory
for a relative minute or two.
Her glory has always been in the mending—
in being the salve, the pumice and the sling.

      Believer of magical kingdoms.
      A wife to Life itself.
      A perpetual eye of the tempest—
      giver of sanctuary to all who come a spiraling.
Keeper of the wisdom a patient life brings.

# Growing Up in a Nuclear World

### *Stinson Anderson*

Total thermo-nuclear annihilation;
It was the rumor of war that I carried in my lunch box
So many times did the Bear and the Eagle square off,
leaving us (me) stepped on and unconscious,
like a dirty penny on the playground,
the dark iron curtain of February clouds closing overhead.

Our school didn't have a fallout shelter,
or even a basement
when such a thing seemed so necessary.
We're doomed, I thought daily.
Red Dawn at the box office,
Cronkite, or Rather it was Jennings.
No matter-their reports of our actor turned cowboy-politician,
standing nose to nose with the Caucasian,
who wore a map of us for a forehead,
only exacerbated my anxiety.

Were all those tornado drills
really about covering up for a tornado?
Because I sure felt insecure,
hunched over like that with my ass exposed.

"Tear down the wall!" played nightly,
and over again during my pre-dawn bus ride to school.
Will somebody push the button?
Or maybe they'll lean on it by accident with a fat elbow,
or spill coffee on it by mistake.

Will someone push the button?
Burn us all tomorrow, but not today, please
because, today I have to hold the line.
Today, the Eagle and the Bear of the school yard
will again stand toe to toe,
like so many recesses before.

When will I not fear the fallout?

---

**Stinson Anderson** lives in North Central Indiana and writes poetry, fiction, and non-fiction. He has been previously published in the *Vignette Review, The Opiate,* and *Memory House.*

## Long Distance Winter
### *Jeff Corey*

I decided to paint my dormant maple,
and went to Home Depot to find
your eye color on a sample card.
You'd called them just plain old green,
but here they were *seedling*.
I asked for a gallon and watched it stir,
rattling like the pop can in my cup holder
for 2,000 miles filling with cigarette butts the last time
I drove away from you.

I poured the paint into the tray and climbed the ladder.
The thin fog was cold aluminum.
I coated the roller.
I extended my arm above the bare, silvery branches,
and gave them enough color to last until it all came back.

# Beachcombing with the Child I'll Probably Never Have
### *Jeff Corey*

You try to lift the bull kelp and because you can't
I grab the tail end and together
we throw it back into the bay because it is also alive.

You search the tide pool while
I plant sand dollars upright in a circle—
a corral for the tiny crab you set inside.

It escapes through a crevice and hides
beneath a rock covered with limpets that breathe
inside their mineral wombs.

The bull kelp reappears atop the carbonated crests,
rising and falling with the incoming waves.
We scatter the sand dollars and you lift the rock

for a last look at the life it shelters
before setting it back in its place
like we were never there.

**Jeff Corey** works both as an adjunct English instructor and landscaper. He resides in Chicago, Illinois.

# Glory

### Mary Hills Kuck

If I go first, I'll take my phone
you know, the pink one
with the little floral strap?

When you reach the glitzy gate
just text to say you're here
and I'll whirl out to meet you.

You'll know me—I'll be in white
like all the rest, but only I
will have that phone.

Take the strap
I'll pull you through
sing glory, glory, glory.

Originally from Illinois, **Mary Hills Kuck** retired from teaching English and Communications, first in the US and for many years in Jamaica, and now lives and walks with her family in the woods in Massachusetts. Her poems have appeared in *Long River Run, Connecticut River Review, Hamden Chronicle, SIMUL: Lutheran Voices in Poetry, Caduceus, The Jamaica Observer, Fire Stick: A Collection of New & Established Caribbean Poets, Fever Grass: A collection of New & Established Caribbean Writers, Massachusetts State Poetry Society, Inc. Anthology,* and *The Aurorean.*

## Alexandra David-Neel

*Michael Lee Johnson*

She edits her life from a room made dark
against a desert dropping summer sun.
A daring traveling Parisian adventurer,
ultimate princess turning toad with age—
snow drops of white in her hair, tiny fingers
thumb joints osteoarthritis
she corrects proofs at 100, pours whiskey,
pours over what she wrote
scribbles notes directed to the future,
applies for a new passport.
With this amount of macular degeneration,
near, monster of writers' approaches,
she wears no spectacles.
Her mind teeters between Himalayas,
distant Gobi Desert.
Running reason through her head for a living,
yet dancing with the youthful world of Cinderella,
she plunges deeper near death into Tibetan mysticism,
trekking across snow covered mountains to Lhasa, Tibet.
Nighttime rest, sleepy face, peeking out that window crack
into the nest, those quiet villages below
tasting a reality beyond her years.

---

**Michael Lee Johnson** lived ten years in Canada during the Vietnam era and is a dual citizen of the United States and Canada. Today he is a poet, freelance writer, amateur photographer, and small business owner in Itasca, Illinois. Mr. Johnson is published in more than one thousand publications. His poems have appeared in 36 countries. He edits and publishes 10 different poetry sites. He was nominated twice for Pushcart Prize 2015; Best of the Net 2016; and twice for Best of the Net 2017. He is the Editor-in-chief of the anthologies *Moonlight Dreamers of Yellow Haze, Dandelion in a Vase of Roses,* and *Warriors with Wings* (out Summer 2018). He also has 161 poetry videos on YouTube: https://www.youtube.com/user/poetrymanusa/videos.

# Children Gathered

### *Douglas G. Campbell*

Children walk
among the ferns of night
cross the long rushing salamander
of a stream
clutching the egg shaped stones
between their toes
fingers squeeze lumps of sugar
an offering to the warm breath
of night's black horses.

Children emerge
from the pores of the forest
collect night's eyes into a bouquet
pull stars from spider's webs
gather night's gifts into baskets
to place among tombs of parents
waiting to be buried.

Children gathered
silent in the meadow's song
grasp the hollow hands of ghosts
lost fathers and mothers
wrapped only in moonlight
they celebrate the death of winter
dancing naked
between the planets and moons
before night dissolves.

# The Promise
### *Douglas G. Campbell*

Dust
clinging like a small child
held sky
dry and rainless

Dust
withering tongues
shriveling words
before they could emerge
as butterflies
within sunlight's dance

Dust
filling wells
following wind's current
where once
water spoke softly
and grass glittered
dew heavy
lithe

Dust
parching dreams
draining promise from a valley.
Frank, my grandfather,
abandoned orchard
hardware store
friends.

Ashes
filtering air
breath collected within nostrils
eyes straining

Ashes
searching for crevices
weak places within us
replacing light
with an argument of crows
scorched discontent

Ashes
where a son had slept
murder transforming
blood to ash
flesh to dust
May, my grandmother,
swaddled by grief
too much pain
dwelling within

Water
an effrontery of color
blooming daily
within reach

Water
cooling wrinkled hands
baptizing gnarled roots
separating rootlets
from ash and dust

Water
living brightly
upon the tongue

**Douglas G. Campbell** lives in Portland, Oregon. He is Professor Emeritus of art at George Fox University where he taught painting, printmaking, drawing and art history courses. He is also the author of *Turning Radius* (2017), *Tree Story* (2018), *Seeing: When Art and Faith Intersect* (2002) and *Parktails* (2012). His poetry and artworks have been published in a number of periodicals including *Harbinger Asylum, Nourish, Off The Coast,* and *Indiana Voice Journal.* His artwork is represented in collections such as The Portland Art Museum, Oregon State University, Ashforth Pacific, Inc. and George Fox University.

# The Container Store
### *Gene Twaronite*

A new store in the mall
promises containers
for every purpose.
Shelves upon shelves
of boxes, bins, and baskets,
tinted jars and shiny canisters
to store everything in your life
and then some.
Such a clever concept—
makes you want to buy new stuff
just to fill those hungry containers.

Maybe someday
they will sell
just the right vessel
to store your thoughts
and emotions in safe
and accessible spaces.

For playful thoughts
tanks and bowls to display
like tropical fish
their gay frolics.

For darker notions
sturdy cages
of glass and steel
to hold them fast
while you study
their motions.

Don't worry about losing
important memories
when you have file cases
of fine-grain oak
or mahogany
to store them securely
by subject and date
against dust, mold,
and the ravages of time.

To show off your finest
thoughts and feelings—
that first love perhaps
or the lost cause
you once fought for—
trophy cabinets
in the living room
when company comes.

For troublesome creatures
that gnaw and consume you—
hate, jealousy, and greed—
killing jars
in matching designer sets.

And for all the mournful memories
never to be forgotten
tasteful urns inscribed with verse
perfect for the mantel.

    [First published by Kelsay Books in *Trash Picker on Mars*, 2016]

# Transformations

## Gene Twaronite

One day, I made a decision and moved the old couch
to the curb, transforming it into trash.

It's the same old couch I always knew
into whose velvety cushions I sank each night
as I ran my hand beneath
in search of free money.

molecules hadn't changed.
The only difference was its value to me.
It had become debased,
no longer the perfect couch.

Back in the old days, if I were an alchemist,
I might have tried turning it into something else
before throwing it away.

Alchemy wasn't just about changing lead into gold.
It involved the belief that everything—
humans, trees, metals, even couches—
is imbued with a living spirit,
each at various stages of divine development.

Since lead was considered a baser metal
and gold the pinnacle of perfection,
alchemists focused on converting lead into gold.
It's also possible they tried turning some old couches
into gold as well. A gold couch—wouldn't that be something?
Of course, a gold couch, though valuable, wouldn't be very comfortable.
One *could* say it had not attained a true state of perfection.

Lead was thought evil because
it had not yet triumphed over its baser nature,
like some people you might know.
The idea was that we must strive
to overcome sin and the forces of darkness,
eventually transforming ourselves
into perfect golden beings.

Catholics have their own kind of alchemy.
They believe that the humble bread and wine
received in communion literally become
different substances—
the body and blood of Jesus Christ,
who is now a part of you.

But I suspect that if you then go out and cheat on your spouse
or swindle thy neighbors out of their retirement funds,
your molecules haven't changed
and you still have a long way to go
to win the gold.

---

**Gene Twaronite's** poems, essays, and short stories have appeared in over forty different print and online magazines, journals, newspapers, and anthologies. He is the author of seven books, including two juvenile novels and two short story collections. His first poetry book *Trash Picker on Mars* was published by Kelsay Books in 2016. His second collection of poems *The Museum of Unwearable Shoes* is scheduled to be released in September 2018. He now resides in Tucson, Arizona. Follow more of Gene's writing at his website https://www.thetwaronitezone.com.

# Missed Opportunity over Coffee
## *Keith Moul*

Our meeting was a fluke, no premeditation at all,
one in a thousand with a dropped cap introduction.

And such a coincidence: we both had developed
a taste for coffee, cream but no sugar: a fortunate
beginning. I thought to know you. As a friend?

The misunderstanding was entirely on my side.

Prepared to discuss other mutual interests, I did
not ask about your politics. When they emerged,
not immediately, but buds of innuendo, shorthand
opinions, confusing allusions to media thinkers,
praises for the rule of law, particularly punitive.

I recoiled. I stood. I apologized; I had to leave.
You called me "doctrinaire." To support this,
you cited as source undisputed alternative facts.

[This poem was first published by *The Pangolin Review*.]

Photo Credit: Ianthe Moul

**Keith Moul**'s poems and photos appear widely. He received his MA from Western Washington, and his PhD from the University of South Carolina. He now lives in Port Angeles, Washington. Finishing Line released his chapbook, *The Future as a Picnic Lunch* in 2015. Aldrich Press published *Naked Among Possibilites* in 2016 and *No Map at Hand* in 2017. Finishing Line published *Investment in Idolatry* in 2017.

# Lifeline
### *Fida Islaih*

Your soul feels lonely
your lifeline wasn't meant to hurt you
it should have been gentle with you.

---

**Fida Islaih** is a poet and editor who lives in Fishers, Indiana

# The End of the Universe, as told by the Building Inspector
### *Steven Shields*

So one day the report lands on my desk that it was time for that abandoned wreck out on highway 18 to come down. You know the one— that dump those investors from Fort Wayne thought they were going to front for the Chinese and make a mint. Never happened, of course. Got it three fourths of the way done and then the shmucks ran out of capital and there it sat for God-knows-how-long. How long? Oh, let's see here (flips pages)...28 billion years, it says. So, a while. And you know how it goes with places like that: First we had to have the sheriff go out there and roust out the bums that had been using it for whatever they were doing in there. Vagrants, the whole bunch of 'em. Drugs. Some nasty mattresses. You know. A pretty sorry mess. They'd propped open a rear-facing door with a rock or something. Some stray dogs in there too, which we rounded up and took to the shelter. So then the demolition guys got in there and did their thing, wiring up the supports with the plastics, all the while not realizing there was one room that got missed somehow that still had a guy lurking in it. Can you believe that?! The bulldozers eventually spotted him, but after the fact. It was too bad, but you know, he shouldn't have been in there in the first place. Let me tell you, I wish I could have seen the look on HIS face when the blast happened.

# Fruitage
## *Steven Shields*

I was the oldest, so of course it was my idea
to climb the red slats of the corn crib,
to perch on its corrugated roof, and survey,
for the last time, our tiny kingdom.

She was gone—mercifully, some said—
not having *been in her right mind for some time*
and so in need of constant care. Now this,
strangers piling out of cars and trucks

along the gravel road, pulling up
behind her ancient Hudson in the muddy
driveway, women picking up and examining,
with a knowing frown, the white ceramic dishpan,

meat grinder, potato masher, some rusty
tools my great-grandfather left behind:
everything going. Everything. And my mother
and her mother, seated at the card table

making change from a metal box, gently
dispensing baked goods and greetings, the Indiana
breeze fingering the hats and trees, waving
the creaky sign beside the road that proclaimed

there'd been a fruit farm there. We swung our legs,
while auctioneers launched fusillades of verbal
rockets, extra noise and syllables aimed
at straw hats and bow ties, at overalls and work boots.

A bored adult cast an occasional eye up
at us while lazily spitting a brown stream,
Mom admonishing us to *get down
from there! If you boys break your fool necks*

*don't ask me to push your wheelchairs!*
About then someone would call her
and she would have to turn away. Meanwhile
the sun warmed the metal beneath our butts

while we pondered the fruit shed, the empty barn,
the fallow field lying to the west

behind the neighbor farmer's barbed wire fence.
In back of us the trees where Worden and Vesta

had made their extra money in season: the cling
peaches, pears and plums; apples good
for canning, mostly, or making applesauce.
At lunch, we scrambled down for chicken, after

which Mom confronted us with a stack of peck
baskets she'd found stashed in a corner of the barn.
*Here, you boys want to climb something,*
*take these out there and make yourselves useful*

*while we clean up,* she said, waving at the orchard,
tall with weeds, rusting implements
looming like monsters from seas of field grass.
*Go pick what you can. Otherwise get over here*

*and help us with these tables and chairs.* Given
*that* choice, we toted tables back
to the church van, watched our elders drift
away to Huntington, Upland or Van Buren.

The day waned. The house was finally closed.
A few things got left behind but not many.
And Mom, the eldest child herself, drove
silently home, the moon racing us

across ripening fields and darkening farms,
heat lightning portraits of silos in sharp relief.
The wind sang Woody Guthrie songs about
the land, but we were in no mood to listen.

---

**Steven Shields** is a native Midwesterner from Marion, Indiana. His careers include all-night FM radio announcer in Indianapolis and many years of broadcast instruction for the University of Wisconsin-Whitewater. His literary work has appeared in such publications as *Angle, Deronda Review, Lyric, Measure, Main Street Rag, Midwestern Gothic, Raintown Review, the Reach of Song, Sleet,* and *Umbrella,* among many others. His debut collection, *Daimonion Sonata,* was published letterpress by Birch Brook (2005). A second collection is forthcoming from Brick Road Poetry Press.

## Modern Apocalypse
*Keith Welch*

Would you recognize the world's end without strange beasts, signs or portents?
Wearing familiar faces, suits and ties the horsemen come forth, all pale and smiling
The end times announced in rousing speeches, before cheering crowds
Hands will be shaken, and terrified babies will be kissed by thin lips
In those times selfishness is virtue and suspicion a civic duty
All agree that sacrifices must be made to achieve perfection of the sacred state
The people will be divided into the loyal and the traitors, each sacrificed in their turn
Shunned, jailed, or gunned down in the darkened streets to protect 'The Children'
Survivors destined to hide from shadow threats in well-armed houses
New enemies supplied daily until minds unable to continue
break under their labor of fear
And the citizens, knowing no allies, savage one another in imagined self-defense
Each seeing the other as though a beast of apocalypse, seven-headed and ten-horned

## Everyone an Action Hero
*Keith Welch*

They say it's just a flesh wound,
as if flesh isn't important anymore.
Bruce Willis takes a bullet
like a bee sting, he kills us
from the screen.   He puts the gun in our hands
outside, boys make finger-guns   bang.

Keanu Reeves is cool, his gun is cool.
I feel it in my hand, its cool weight.
The more men he kills, the cooler it becomes.
The faster he kills, the cooler we become.
The men want to be James Bond, who kills
and fucks, fucks and kills.

Action movie heroes are killing the self,
the self that respects death.
The bodies pile up, they have to be
carted away to where their mothers can
see them. There are no mothers in action movies.
Mothers don't kill, they cry, such a downer.
Mothers would kill the vibe.

# Alien Intervention
## Keith Welch

Aliens have come to Earth!
They cluck and shake
their heads(?), that our
parents have left us
alone to make such a mess.

From orbit, they laugh:
"Look, the ones in suits
think they're important!"
"So adorable!"

Our wars look like ants
fighting over wasteland.
They think it must be
a sport, since we love
it so much.

They leave a message
on the moon for when
the adults come home:
"Please call us at
your earliest convenience.
It's about your children."

---

**Keith Welch** lives in Bloomington, Indiana where he works at the Indiana University Herman B. Wells Library. He has poems published in *Open: Journal of Arts and Letters, Writers Resist, Dime Show Review, Every Pigeon,* and *Literary Orphans.* When he's not writing for publication, he specializes in political epigrams. He loves to have contact with other poets and invites everyone to follow him on Twitter at @Outraged_Poet.

# Seven Places for the Soul
### *Kyle Clark*

a glass case
with its patient red axe.

a music box
with its out-of-tune twinkle
sopping up baby's
blue.

a vase
with its daffodils
cut
two inches too short.

a poem
with its overdrawn drama
sprawling naked
in its vegetable garden.

a farmhouse
with each of its barren rooms
filling steadily with armoires
which are filling steadily
themselves.

a bottle
with its crimson voodoo
fervently corked inside.

a fist
full of change
entreating a jukebox
to waste it.

---

**Kyle Clark** lives and works in Carmel, Indiana. He is a founding editor of Indiana University Kokomo's *Field: A Journal of Arts and Sciences*, and his work appears or is forthcoming in *The Labyrinth, Tributaries, Manuscripts*, and elsewhere.

# Custody
## Kristin Capezio

We call it your weekend
Every other and a week in the summer
Mom watches at the tattered screen
her eyes set on black
a bold yellow line dividing the
comers and the goers.
You are a comer. Soon, a goer.
We are giddy sisters, firecrackers
fighting on the living room floor
energy uncontained, ears acute to the
motor of a tired Ford Bronco—the low squeal of brakes
the drip of the exhaust on the hot asphalt
while we wait, exhaling tedious energy.
you said half past two or so
its seven
Mom unlocks the screen. The truck door creeks; slams shut
You are our blue jean hero. Our all-American dad.
The porch fills with Stetson and ash, face unshaven, dwindling sun light
coming through your curled red hair. A halo, a glowing fire offset by oceanic windows
to the soul.

Our bags behind our backs we stand at attention; frenzied, undone.
Mom's eyes do not soften. They bend into you, bend into us.
She speaks softly. Waits with eyes pushing the weight of the old oak table forward
You are talking quickly but politely, scribbling numbers on a page
You leave for her this tiny rectangle
an exchange that turns hard eyes soft.
She smiles and waves goodbye. The weekend. Together we are free.

But are you?

---

**Kristin Capezio,** resident of Massachusetts, is a longtime lover of poetry and has had submissions accepted at *Tipton Poetry Journal* in the past. She believes that poetry creates a mood around an experience, a point in time. Her poetry reflects that position. The experiences she has had changed the way she views the world. In the retelling of these experiences through poetry, she believes poets give readers a glimpse into their inner lives, or at least, the inner life they wish to present.

## Gaius Cassius Longinus Breaks the Fourth Wall
*Tim Hawkins*

—After Shakespeare's *Julius Caesar (I, ii)*

Another lapse in reason at the top
Displaying yet more hubris than the last.
We've grown exhausted asking to what depths
This Caesar may sink before he's called to task
To answer for his rancid petulance.
The Grand Old Party leaders have decamped
From bully pulpits where they might stand tall
Like Antony, who with one heartfelt speech
Turned all of Rome against our noble band.
*So are they all, all honourable men…*

The boss, meanwhile, sounds out his entourage
Whose murmurings plumb the depths of his just cause.
Not for the first time wonder strikes me dumb
As I consider just how much is lost.
*Why, man, he doth bestride the narrow world*
Where he, alone, is master of our fates.
Yet, needlessly, he circumscribes that orb
To circumnavigate with baby steps.

*Now, in the names of all the gods at once,*
*Upon what meat do these our Caesars feed,*
*That they are grown so great? Age, thou art shamed…*
By harlequins who play the role of kings.
Tell me again what brought us to this place
Where narrow interests forge a brittle peace
That propagates unnatural human states
By prying man from gods and young from old?
Where families fly apart like airborne seeds
And in the windswept darkness take up root.
On this, like so much else, the pundits clash
With wars of words torn from the holy books,
While alienated men retreat to caves
To write God's name in smoke across the skies.
Great Caesar has no answer, just more Tweets,
Yet Caesar wields a rudimentary tool:
The wedge that drives our citizens apart.

# A Brush with Royalty
## Tim Hawkins

Somehow, by the time I bothered to look up
it was almost spring again
and most of us had survived the winter,
though last year it had seemed there were pines as far as the eye could see,
and I remembered something about a chickadee.

But then I caught the pear tree at full glance.
And at once, as if shrugging off the season's hold,
as if looking back centuries, it was autumn's final day again
or winter's first, and I found as I fondled the tree's final offering
of the season, that inside the split, frost-puckered skin of that pear,
its pulpy flesh was gaudily alive with shimmering sequins
blazing with warmth and light.

In the way they kept their own counsel and disdained my proffered hand,
I felt I had discovered something akin to beleaguered aristocrats
and their last vestige of a more regal way of life:
a full retinue of ladybugs squired by a final squadron of wasps
each keeping to its own distinct lobe, yet preparing, nonetheless,
to winter together in that hovel of shriveled fruit.

At the core of this most succulent of fruits grown overripe,
I had the fleeting notion of abdicating royalty in flight
and the sensation of finding something precious
like a Faberge egg mislaid among all of the looting;

And of peering into it against a backdrop of gray and desolate boulevards
leading out past a parade ground of wind-chapped and ill-fed recruits
going through the motions of a drill,

a grim and silent rehearsal
for totalitarian winter's
seemingly offhand regicide.

---

**Tim Hawkins** has lived and traveled widely throughout North America, Southeast Asia, Europe, and Latin America, where he has worked as a journalist, technical writer, communications manager, and teacher in international schools. His writing has appeared in *Blueline, Eclectica, The Flea, Iron Horse Literary Review, The Midwest Quarterly, The Pedestal Magazine,* and *Verse Wisconsin.* He has been nominated twice for a Pushcart Prize (2011, 2017) and was chosen to serve as preliminary judge for the 47th Annual Dyer-Ives Poetry Competition (2015) judged by Mark Doty. His poetry collection, *Wanderings at Deadline,* was published in 2012 by Aldrich Press. Tim lives in Michigan. Read more at www.timhawkinspoetry.com.

# Premonition, 1964
## Greg Field

*Good Friday Earthquake,*
*Anchorage, Alaska*

We played on ice bergs,
leaped from one blue giant
to another as they bobbed
and dipped in gray water.
I called out to my friend
how unsteady the blue world
was beneath the leaden sky.

I saw houses shift
and tumble into the bay
where blue ice bergs,
house-sized sat stranded
by the receding tide
in the rolling mud.

I learned my friend fell
through his funneled floor,
his house collapsed
onto his curled form.
I saw his rooftop
submerged in clay.
Blue ice bergs advanced
in the shifting bay.

---

**Greg Field** is a writer, artist, musician, and sailor. He plays in the band *River Cow Orchestra,* a totally improvisational jazz group and in the band *Brother Iota,* a space/rock music group. He has a BFA and an MA in painting and his paintings are in several private collections around the country. His poems have been published in many journals and anthologies  including *New Letters, Laurel Review, Chiron Review, Flint Hills Review.* His book *The Longest Breath* (MidAmerica Press) was a Thorpe Menn Finalist. His new book, released from Mammoth Press is *Black Heart,* which focuses on his Native American heritage. He lives in Independence, Missouri with his wife, poet Maryfrances Wagner and their dog, Sylvia Plath.

## The Editors

### Editor

**Barry Harris** is editor of the *Tipton Poetry Journal* and two anthologies by Brick Street Poetry: *Mapping the Muse: A Bicentennial Look at Indiana Poetry* and *Words and Other Wild Things*. He has published one poetry collection, *Something At The Center*. Barry lives in Brownsburg, Indiana and is retired from Eli Lilly and Company. His poetry has appeared in *Kentucky Review, Valparaiso Poetry Review, Grey Sparrow, Silk Road Review, Saint Ann's Review, Boston Literary Magazine, Night Train, Silver Birch Press, Flying Island, Awaken Consciousness, Writers' Bloc*, and *Red-Headed Stepchild*. One of his poems was on display at the National Museum of Sport and another is painted on a barn in Boone County, Indiana as part of Brick Street Poetry's Word Hunger public art project. His poems are also included in these anthologies: *From the Edge of the Prairie; Motif 3: All the Livelong Day;* and *Twin Muses: Art and Poetry*.

### Assistant Editor

**Kylie Seitz** is assistant editor of the *Tipton Poetry Journal*, as well as Editor-in-Chief of *Etchings Literary and Fine Arts Magazine* at the University of Indianapolis. Despite being a double major in creative writing and professional writing at the University of Indianapolis, Kylie spends far too much of her time actively avoiding any actual writing, academic or otherwise. As such, she is currently mastering the arts of baking banana bread, sliding in her fluffy socks on hardwood floor (and sometimes the university's tile hallways), and pulling sumo for deadlift.

*Tipton Poetry Journal*

## *Contributor Biographies*

**Stinson Anderson** lives in North Central Indiana and writes poetry, fiction, and non-fiction. He has been previously published in the *Vignette Review, The Opiate,* and *Memory House.*

**Judy Shepps Battle** has been writing essays and poems long before retiring from being a psychotherapist and sociology professor. She is a New Jersey resident, addictions specialist, consultant, and freelance writer. Her poems have been accepted in a variety of publications, including *Ascent Aspirations; Barnwood Press; Battered Suitcase; Caper Literary Journal; Epiphany Magazine; Joyful; Message in a Bottle Poetry Magazine; Raleigh Review; Rusty Truck; Short, Fast and Deadly; Tishman Review;* and *Wilderness House Literary Press.*

**Daniel Bourne's** books include *The Household Gods* (Cleveland State) and *Where No One Spoke the Language* (CustomWords). His poems have also been in such journals as *Field, Ploughshares, American Poetry Review, Conduit, Boulevard, Guernica, Salmagundi, Yale Review, Pleiades, Quarterly West, Willow Springs, Witness, Shenandoah, Prairie Schooner, Plume, New Letters, Indiana Review, Many Mountains Moving,* and *Cimarron Review.* The recipient of four Ohio Arts Council poetry fellowships, he teaches in the English Department and in the Environmental Studies Program at The College of Wooster in Ohio, where he edits *Artful Dodge,* a magazine of American fiction, poetry, and essay with a special interest in both place and literature in translation.

**Douglas G. Campbell** lives in Portland, Oregon. He is Professor Emeritus of art at George Fox University where he taught painting, printmaking, drawing and art history courses. He is also the author of *Turning Radius* (2017), *Tree Story* (2018), *Seeing: When Art and Faith Intersect* (2002) and *Parktails* (2012). His poetry and artworks have been published in a number of periodicals including *Harbinger Asylum, Nourish, Off The Coast,* and *Indiana Voice Journal.* His artwork is represented in collections such as The Portland Art Museum, Oregon State University, Ashforth Pacific, Inc. and George Fox University.

**Kristin Capezio,** resident of Massachusetts, is a longtime lover of poetry and has had submissions accepted at *Tipton Poetry Journal* in the past. She believes that poetry creates a mood around an experience, a point in time. Her poetry reflects that position. The experiences she has had changed the way she views the world. In the retelling of these experiences through poetry, she believes poets give readers a glimpse into their inner lives, or at least, the inner life they wish to present.

**Kyle Clark** lives and works in Carmel, Indiana. He is a founding editor of Indiana University Kokomo's *Field: A Journal of Arts and Sciences,* and his work appears or is forthcoming in *The Labyrinth, Tributaries, Manuscripts,* and elsewhere.

**Joan Colby** has published widely in journals such as *Poetry, Atlanta Review, South Dakota Review, New York Quarterly,* and *Prairie Schooner*. Awards include two Illinois Arts Council Literary Awards, Rhino Poetry Award, and an Illinois Arts Council Fellowship in Literature. She was a finalist in the GSU Poetry Contest (2007) and Nimrod International Pablo Neruda Prize (2009, 2012) and received honorable mentions in the *North American Review*'s James Hearst Poetry Contest (2008, 2010). She is the editor of *Illinois Racing News,* associate editor of *Kentucky Review* and *FutureCycle Press,* and lives on a small horse farm in Northern Illinois. She has published 11 books including *The Lonely Hearts Killers, The Atrocity Book,* and her newest book from *Future Cycle Press—Dead Horses*. FutureCycle has just published *Selected Poems*. Her book, *Ribcage*, won the 2015 Kithara Book Prize from Glass Lyre Press.

**Gayle Compton,** a hillbilly from Eastern Kentucky, lives up the river from where Randall McCoy is buried and attended college on the hill where "Cotton Top" Mounts was hanged. With deep affection, he tells the story of Appalachia's common people, allowing them to speak, without apology, in their own colorful language. His prize-winning stories, poems, and essays have appeared most recently in *Sow's Ear, Now and Then, New Southerner, Blue Collar Review, Kentucky Review,* and *Main Street Rag* anthologies. *Coal Dust and Crabgrass,* a collection of poetry, is due March 2017 from FutureCycle Press.

**Jeff Corey** works both as an adjunct English instructor and landscaper. He resides in Chicago, Illinois.

**Brett Cortelletti** is a senior at Malone University in Canton, Ohio majoring in English Language Arts. He has served as an editor for *The Quaker*, Malone's online literary journal. In addition to being a reader and a writer, he is also a competitive long-distance runner. Most recently, his work has appeared in *The Cobalt Review* and *The Tulane Review*.

**Gareth Culshaw** lives in Wales. He has his first collection coming out in 2018 by futurecycle. And he is encouraged by his best friend, his collie, Jasper.

**Michael Estabrook** is retired and living in Massachusetts. No more useless meetings under florescent lights in stuffy windowless rooms, able instead to focus on making better poems when he's not, of course, endeavoring to satisfy his wife's legendary Honey-Do List. His latest collection of poems is *Bouncy House*, edited by Larry Fagin (Green Zone Editions, 2016).

**Greg Field** is a writer, artist, musician, and sailor. He plays in the band *River Cow Orchestra*, a totally improvisational jazz group and in the band *Brother Iota,* a space/rock music group. He has a BFA and an MA in painting and his paintings are in several private collections around the country. His poems have been published in many journals and anthologies including *New Letters, Laurel Review, Chiron Review, Flint Hills Review*. His book *The Longest Breath* (MidAmerica Press) was a Thorpe Menn Finalist. His new book, released from Mammoth Press is *Black Heart*, which focuses on his Native American heritage. He lives in Independence, Missouri with his wife, poet Maryfrances Wagner and their dog, Sylvia Plath.

**Donald Gasperson** has a Bachelor of Science degree in Psychology from the University of Washington and a Master of Arts degree in Clinical Psychology from Pepperdine University. He has worked primarily as a psychiatric rehabilitation counselor. He writes as an exercise in physical, mental and spiritual health. He has been published or has been accepted for publication by *Five Willows Literary Review, Poetry Pacific, Three Line Poetry, Quail Bell Magazine* and *Big Windows Review*. He lives in Klamath Falls, Oregon.

**Tim Hawkins** has lived and traveled widely throughout North America, Southeast Asia, Europe, and Latin America, where he has worked as a journalist, technical writer, communications manager, and teacher in international schools. His writing has appeared in *Blueline, Eclectica, The Flea, Iron Horse Literary Review, The Midwest Quarterly, The Pedestal Magazine,* and *Verse Wisconsin*. He has been nominated twice for a Pushcart Prize (2011, 2017) and was chosen to serve as preliminary judge for the 47th Annual Dyer-Ives Poetry Competition (2015) judged by Mark Doty. His poetry collection, *Wanderings at Deadline*, was published in 2012 by Aldrich Press. Tim lives in Michigan. Read more at www.timhawkinspoetry.com.

**Fida Islaih** is a poet and editor who lives in Fishers, Indiana

**Dan Jacoby** is a graduate of St. Louis University, Chicago State University, and Governors State University, currently residing in Illinois. He has published poetry in *Anchor and Plume (Kindred), Arkansas Review, Belle Reve Literary Journal, Bombay Gin, Burningword Literary Review, Canary, The Fourth River, Wilderness House Literary Review, Steel Toe Review, The American Journal of Poetry,* and *Red Fez* to name a few. He is a former educator, steel worker, and army spook. He is a member of the Carlinville Writers Guild and was nominated for a Pushcart Prize in 2015. He is currently looking for a publisher for a collection of poetry.

**Michael Lee Johnson** lived ten years in Canada during the Vietnam era and is a dual citizen of the United States and Canada. Today he is a poet, freelance writer, amateur photographer, and small business owner in Itasca, Illinois. Mr. Johnson is published in more than one thousand publications. His poems have appeared in 36 countries. He edits and publishes 10 different poetry sites. He was nominated twice for Pushcart Prize 2015; Best of the Net 2016; and twice for Best of the Net 2017. He is the Editor-in-chief of the anthologies *Moonlight Dreamers of Yellow Haze, Dandelion in a Vase of Roses,* and *Warriors with Wings* (out Summer 2018). He also has 161 poetry videos on YouTube: https://www.youtube.com/user/poetrymanusa/videos.

**Michael Keshigian**, from New Hampshire, had his twelfth poetry collection, *Into The Light*, released in April, 2017 by Flutter Press. He has been published in numerous national and international journals, including *Oyez Review, Red River Review, Sierra Nevada College Review, Oklahoma Review,* and *Chiron Review,* and has appeared as feature writer in over a twenty publications with 6 Pushcart Prize and 2 Best Of The Net nominations.

**Connie Kingman** is founder of Prairie Writers Guild and serves as managing editor for the Guild's anthology, *From the Edge of the Prairie*. She is a lifetime resident of Rensselaer, Indiana.

# Tipton Poetry Journal

**John P. Kristofco**, from Highland Heights, Ohio, is professor of English and the former dean of Wayne College in Orrville, Ohio. His poetry, short stories, and essay have appeared in over a hundred different publications, including *Folio, Cimarron Review, Nerve Cowboy, Rattle, Poem,* and *Sierra Nevada Review.* He has published three collections of poetry—*A Box of Stones, Apparitions,* and *The Fire in Our Eyes*—and has been nominated for the Pushcart Prize five times.

**Judy Kronenfeld** is the author of six collections of poetry including *Bird Flying through the Banquet* (FutureCycle, 2017), *Shimmer* (WordTech, 2012), and *Light Lowering in Diminished Sevenths* (Antrim House, 2012)—winner of the 2007 Litchfield Review Poetry Book Prize. Her poems have been in *Calyx, Cider Press Review, Cimarron Review, Hiram Poetry Review, Natural Bridge, The Pedestal, Valparaiso Poetry Review, The Women's Review of Books, Rattle,* and in more than twenty anthologies. She is Lecturer Emerita, Creative Writing Department, University of California, Riverside, and an Associate Editor of the online poetry journal, *Poemeleon.*

Originally from Illinois, **Mary Hills Kuck** retired from teaching English and Communications, first in the US and for many years in Jamaica, and now lives and walks with her family in the woods in Massachusetts. Her poems have appeared in *Long River Run, Connecticut River Review, Hamden Chronicle, SIMUL: Lutheran Voices in Poetry, Caduceus, The Jamaica Observer, Fire Stick: A Collection of New & Established Caribbean Poets, Fever Grass: A collection of New & Established Caribbean Writers, Massachusetts State Poetry Society, Inc. Anthology,* and *The Aurorean.*

**Doris Lynch** has recent work in this journal as well as *Frogpond, Flying Island, Haibun Today,* and the *Atlanta Review.* She won three Indiana individual artist's grants, and last year won the Genjuan International Haibun Award. She currently resides in Bloomington, Indiana.

**Marianne Lyon** has been a music teacher for 39 years. After teaching in Hong Kong she returned to the Napa Valley and has been published in various literary magazines and reviews. She has spent time teaching in Nicaragua. She is a member of the California Writers Club, Healdsburg Literary Guild. She is an Adjunct Professor at Touro University.

A resident of New York, **Stephen Mead** is an Outsider multi-media artist and writer. Since the 1990s he's been grateful to many editors for publishing his work in print zines and eventually online. He is also grateful to have managed to keep various day jobs for the Health Insurance. In 2014 he began a webpage to gather links of his poetry being published in such zines as *Great Works, Unlikely Stories, Quill & Parchment,* etc., in one place: Poetry on the Line, Stephen Mead.

**Karla Linn Merrifield,** a nine-time Pushcart-Prize nominee and National Park Artist-in-Residence, has had 600+ poems appear in dozens of journals and anthologies. She has 12 books to her credit, the newest of which is *Bunchberries, More Poems of Canada, a sequel to Godwit: Poems of Canada* (FootHills), which received the Eiseman Award for Poetry. Forthcoming this fall is *Psyche's Scroll,* a full-length poem, published by The Poetry Box Selects. She is assistant editor and poetry book reviewer for The Centrifugal Eye and lives in Brockport, New York. Visit her blog, Vagabond Poet Redux, at http://karlalinn.blogspot.com.

**George Moore** now lives on the south shore of Nova Scotia. Recent poetry collections include *Saint Agnes Outside the Walls* (FutureCycle 2016) and *Children's Drawings of the Universe* (Salmon Poetry 2015). Publications include the *Atlantic, North American Review, Poetry,* and *Colorado Review.*

**Keith Moul**'s poems and photos appear widely. He received his MA from Western Washington, and his PhD from the University of South Carolina. He now lives in Port Angeles, Washington. Finishing Line released his chapbook, *The Future as a Picnic Lunch* in 2015. Aldrich Press published *Naked Among Possibilites* in 2016 and *No Map at Hand* in 2017. Finishing Line published *Investment in Idolatry* in 2017.

**William Page's** fifth collection of poems, *In this Maybe Best of All Possible Worlds*, won the 2016 Poetry Book Award from FutureCycle Press. His *Bodies Not Our Own* (Memphis State University Press) received the Walter R. Smith Distinguished Book Award. His poems have appeared widely in such journals as *The North American Review, The Southern Review, Southern Poetry Review, Wisconsin Review, Ploughshares, The Midwest Quarterly, The Sewanee Review,* and *Valparaiso Poetry Review* and in a number of anthologies, most recently in *The Southern Poetry Anthology, Volume VI*. His poetry has been featured in the Best of the Net and nominated for the Pushcart Prize. He is founding editor of *The Pinch* and lives in Memphis, Tennessee.

**Akshaya Pawaskar** is a doctor practicing in India, and poetry is her passion. Her poems have been published in *Tipton Poetry Journal, Writer's Ezine, Efiction India, Ink Drift, The Blue Nib, Her heart poetry, Awake in the world* anthology by Riverfeet Press, and a few anthologies by Lost Tower publications. She had been chosen as 'Poet of the week' on *Poetry Superhighway* and featured writer in *Wordweavers* poetry contest.

**Simon Perchik** is an attorney whose poems have appeared in *Partisan Review, The New Yorker, Tipton Poetry Journal* and elsewhere. He resides in East Hampton, New York.

**Timothy Pilgrim,** a Pacific Northwest poet with over 410 acceptances by journals such as *Seattle Review, Cirque, San Pedro River Review, Toasted Cheese, Windsor Review, Tipton Poetry Journal,* and *Third Wednesday,* is author of *Mapping water* (Flying Trout Press, 2016) and co-author of *Bellingham poems* (2014). His work is at www.timothypilgrim.org.

**Timothy Robbin**s teaches ESL. He has a B.A. in French and an M.A. in Applied Linguistics. His poems have appeared in *Three New Poets, Slant, Main Street Rag, Adelaide Literary Magazine, Off The Coas*t and others. His collection *Denny's Arbor Vitae* was published in 2017. He lives with his husband of twenty years in Kenosha, Wisconsin, birthplace of Orson Welles.

**Stephen R. Roberts** collects books, gargoyles, poetic lariats, and various other obstacles that fit into his basic perceptions of a chaotic and twisted world that pays scant attention to him as far as he knows. He's been published in *Alembic, Briar Cliff Review, Borderlands, Willow Springs, Karamu, Water-Stone, Bryant Literary Review, Yalobusha Review*, and many others. His full length collection, *Almost Music From Between Places*, is available from Chatter House Press. Stephen lives in Westfield, Indiana.

# *Tipton Poetry Journal*

**Steven Shields** is a native Midwesterner from Marion, Indiana. His careers include all-night FM radio announcer in Indianapolis and many years of broadcast instruction for the University of Wisconsin-Whitewater. His literary work has appeared in such publications as *Angle, Deronda Review, Lyric, Measure, Main Street Rag, Midwestern Gothic, Raintown Review, the Reach of Song, Sleet,* and *Umbrella,* among many others. His debut collection, *Daimonion Sonata,* was published letterpress by Birch Brook (2005). A second collection is forthcoming from Brick Road Poetry Press.

**Allison Thorpe's** new chapbook is *The Shepherds of Tenth Avenue* (forthcoming from Finishing Line Press). Recent work appears in *Pleiades, Appalachian Heritage, Stonecoast Review, Solidago, Still: The Journal,* and *Roanoke Review.* She lives in Lexington, Kentucky.

**Gene Twaronite's** poems, essays, and short stories have appeared in over forty different print and online magazines, journals, newspapers, and anthologies. He is the author of seven books, including two juvenile novels and two short story collections. His first poetry book *Trash Picker on Mars* was published by Kelsay Books in 2016. His second collection of poems *The Museum of Unwearable Shoes* is scheduled to be released in September 2018. He now resides in Tucson, Arizona. Follow more of Gene's writing at his website https://www.thetwaronitezone.com.

**Deborah Walker** began writing poetry in 2012 after she and her husband moved from the city to a log cabin on sixty acres. She is a member of the Ohio Poetry Association, and her work has also appeared in its annual journal *Common Threads.*

**Keith Welch** lives in Bloomington, Indiana where he works at the Indiana University Herman B. Wells Library. He has poems published in *Open: Journal of Arts and Letters, Writers Resist, Dime Show Review, Every Pigeon,* and *Literary Orphans.* When he's not writing for publication, he specializes in political epigrams. He loves to have contact with other poets and invites everyone to follow him on Twitter at @Outraged_Poet.

**Evan D. Williams's** poetry has appeared in *Borderlands, IthacaLit, Mud Season Review, Penned Parenthood,* and *Stillwater.* He is an art appraiser by vocation and lives with his wife in the foothills of the Appalachians in New York State.

**Barry Yeoman** is originally from Springfield, Ohio and currently lives and writes in London, Ohio. His work has appeared, or is forthcoming in *Mission at Tenth, Common Ground Review, Right Hand Pointing, Crack the Spine, Harbinger Asylum,* and *Broad River Review,* among other print and online journals. More of his work can be found at https://www.redfez.net/editArtworks.

Made in the USA
Middletown, DE
05 June 2018